Goal Setting

CONFIDENCE + GOALS = SUCCESS

$$C + G = S$$

Don Wicker, Ph.D.

authorHOUSE®

AuthorHouse™
1663 Liberty Drive, Suite 200
Bloomington, IN 47403
www.authorhouse.com
Phone: 1-800-839-8640

First published by AuthorHouse 6/3/2008

ISBN: 978-1-4343-8950-3 (sc)
ISBN: 978-1-4343-8951-0 (hc)

Printed in the United States of America
Bloomington, Indiana

This book is printed on acid-free paper.

Biography

Dr. Wicker has been teaching at numerous colleges and universities since 1999. As a full-time college professor his areas of concentration include the following: Organizational Behavior, Business Ethics, Operations Management, Quality Management, International Management, and Information Technology Management.

Dr. Wicker's educational background includes a Doctoral degree in the area of Business Organization & Management from Capella University – Minneapolis, Minnesota. Masters of Science degree in Business Administration from Central Michigan University – Mt. Pleasant, Michigan, and a Bachelors of Science degree in Business from Northern Michigan University – Marquette, Michigan.

His business experience includes 21 years

working in the automotive industry for General Motors Corporation. During his career with General Motors his work experience included assignments in: Accounting, Auditing, Finance, Vehicle Sales Service & Marketing, and Service Parts Operations.

CONFIDENCE + GOALS = SUCCESS

$$C + G = S$$

GOAL-SETTING TECHNIQUES

By Don Wicker, Ph.D.

Professor – Brazosport College

Copyright 1993, 2005, 2006, 2008

2nd Edition

Author House Publishing

Table of Contents

What Are Goals?

Goals – Goals – Goals. What are goals? Goals are future outcomes that individuals and groups desire and strive to achieve. The goal-setting process is one of the most unique and important motivational tools for affecting the performance of an individual.

Why Are Goals Important?

Research tells us that goals are important because of five basic reasons:

1. Goals guide and direct behavior.

2. Goals provide challenges.

3. Goals justify the performance.

4. Goals define the basis for strategy.

5. Goals serve an organizing function.

Goals in Life

Why can't people achieve their goals in life? This question has been researched for years; however, the answer has never been clearly defined until now. Through my research, I have determined that a lack of planning prevents people from achieving their goals.

In Webster's Dictionary, a *goal* is defined as the place at which a race, or a trip, has ended—an end that one strives to attain, the place over or into which the ball or puck must go to score. The C + G = S philosophy tells us that goals are defined as a desired pattern or action that leads to specific successful results.

C + G = S also tells us that goals need to be planned. Goals cannot begin by themselves, which is how the C + G = S philosophy started. My research determined that confidence and planning were key factors in goal-setting techniques. The word *confidence,* as defined by Webster's Dictionary, is the belief in one's own ability. *Success* is defined as a favorable result—the gaining of wealth, fame, and accomplishments. The definitions listed in Webster's Dictionary of each key word helped develop the acronym: C + G = S (Confidence + Goals = Success).

Success is a journey that starts when we decide to try to accomplish something. It arrives in all shapes and sizes. Examples include obtaining an "A" on a test, winning a baseball game, or completing a school project. Positive results signal success.

The word *confidence* in our philosophy is connected to goals and success. Confidence is the result of having obtained different accomplishments throughout life. Confidence starts when we are born; for example, before babies can learn how to walk, they fall down. Each day a baby tries to walk, the rate of falling down decreases, and his or her confidence increases. With this increase in confidence and decrease in falling down, most babies eventually start walking.

Dr. Wicker's Goal Chart

$$C + G = S$$

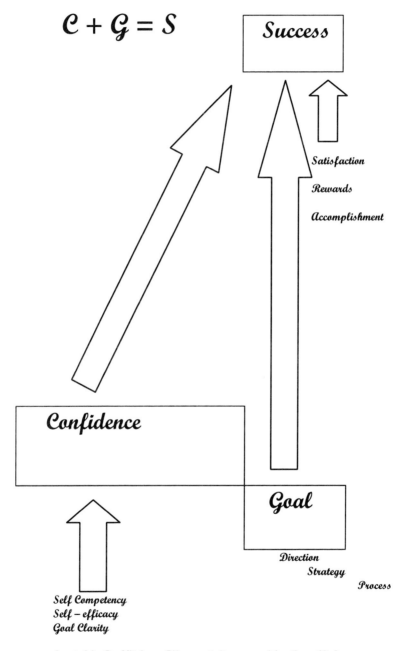

Success

Satisfaction

Rewards

Accomplishment

Confidence

Goal

Direction

Strategy

Process

Self Competency
Self – efficacy
Goal Clarity

Goal Setting

Goal setting is the most important initiative that takes place in a person's life. Goals should be established, planned, and reviewed annually.

I would like to share a personal experience concerning gaining confidence at an early age. When I was ten years old, my mother enrolled me into Little League baseball, which was a game that I really enjoyed playing. Playing the game of baseball allowed me to gain confidence in myself, and it helped me believe in my abilities. Filled with an abundance of ingrained confidence, I was not afraid to engage in other sport activities. I truly believed in my abilities, mainly because of the confidence I had obtained. Setting goals to become proficient in other sports was easy, due to the confidence-builders that I received during my Little League baseball experience.

Recognizing the steps that were taken in achieving past accomplishments will amaze the average person. We all have used some form of goal setting in our lives. A good example of goal setting for the average person originates with a simple task such as learning to read.

The ability to read is not a skill that people are born with; it is a learned behavior. However, most people can remember practicing and teaching themselves how to read. They did not realize it during this phase of learning, but they were in the process of setting goals to learn how to read. For example, most people try to increase their reading speed continuously every day, while others try to increase their comprehension of words. These examples help us to understand how learning to read was a process of goal setting. The $C + G = S$ philosophy was utilized, but it was not readily apparent.

Dr. Wicker's Performance Scale

What is the impact of Goals on our daily performance?

When Goals	Achievement will be
Are clear and specific	Higher
Are vague and unclear	Lower
Involve rewards	Higher
Have no rewards	Lower
Have been accepted	Higher
Have been rejected	Lower
Are set by you	Higher
Are challenging	Higher
Are easy and boring	Lower

$C + G = S$ *Defined*

The CONFIDENCE + GOALS = SUCCESS philosophy was utilized early in life while learning how to read.

CONFIDENCE – People can read, which allows a person to
    believe that reading is possible.
GOALS – Each day while reading, a person attempts to
    increase reading speed and comprehension.
SUCCESS – This occurs when a person can read with clarity
    and comprehension of material has been achieved.

As illustrated through this example, goal setting has and always will be a part of our everyday lives. The Goal Setting can be utilized by anyone to learn how to set goals.

List 10 Accomplishments During the Past Year

1. _____

2. _____

3. _____

4. _____

5. _____

6. _____

7. _____

8. _____

9. _____

10. _____

Notes

List 10 Things You Need to Improve About Yourself

1. _____

2. _____

3. _____

4. _____

5. _____

6. _____

7. _____

8. _____

9. _____

10. _____

Notes

List 10 Goals You Want to Accomplish This Year

1. _____

2. _____

3. _____

4. _____

5. _____

6. _____

7. _____

8. _____

9. _____

10. _____

Your Signature Here: _____

Notes

Analyzing Goal Outcomes

If you have completed the goal-setting exercises, the next step is to analyze the outcomes of your goals. You should answer the following questions by reviewing how you believe your goal outcomes will transpire.

Notes

Evidence of Goals

What do you see? _____

_____

_____

What do you hear? _____

_____

_____

What do you feel? _____

_____

_____

Notes

Assistance

Who helped you achieve your goal? _____

_____

_____

_____

_____

_____

_____

_____

_____

_____

_____

_____

_____

Notes

Goal Verification

How will you know the goal has been achieved?

_____

_____

_____

What person or persons will be happy about your accomplish-

ments?

_____

_____

_____

Was goal setting a successful process?

_____

_____

_____

Notes

Does Goal Setting Work

Does goal setting really work? We can all recite stories about how we have achieved goals in the past. However, when taking a closer look into the goal-setting process, some startling facts are revealed. When I talk about the term 'goal setting' I am referring to writing your objective or goals on a sheet of paper. I have found throughout my research that people do not take ownership of their goals until they become reality, meaning writing it down so they can see it on paper. When people write about their goals, they take ownership of an idea and process. Basically, by recording their objectives on paper, it turns an abstract idea into a concrete, tangible reality. Making your objectives or goals become reality by writing them down allows others to view what you have written, and gives you a psychological contract with those who see your goals. They become your partner in goal setting, reminding you about the goals you have set for yourself.

Great examples of goal setting and having a psychological contract with others happened very early in my life. When I enrolled in college during 1984, my goal was to finish my studies within 4 years. I set my standards high; therefore, I wrote my 4-year goal on a note card and began showing my parents, relatives, and friends my very aggressive goal. I stated that my goal was aggressive because of one main reason – when I arrived on my college campus, I found out that the average student earned her / his degree in 5 to 6 years. The timeline I set for myself was 4 years, lower than my school's average; however, I was not going to retract my statement. Besides, relatives and friends would have taken a retraction of my goals as a sign of failure. A signal of failure would have generated negative thoughts and discussions by the people that needed to encourage me.

My first year in college was very challenging. I received excellent grades, but I needed to drop one class to maintain my honor status. Honor status increased the level of expectations from parents, relatives, and friends. Everyone simply expected me to graduate based on my first year results. After talking with other students that were juniors and seniors, I quickly realized that dropping classes to maintain a high grade point average would prolong my college stay. I talked with students who informed me that dropping classes extended their stay by 1 or 2 years. I could not imagine telling my parents, relatives, and friends that I would be graduating in 6 years, not 4 as I originally stated.

Since my first year in college consisted of excellent grades and one dropped class, I realized that drastic action had to be taken to maintain my goal of graduating in 4 years. After the school year was over, my action plan involved enrolling in summer school at my university, at my own expense. How was I going to pay for summer school since I was basically like other students, broke! With no prospect of paying for summer school, I resorted to selling the one thing I did have to sell, my car. I leased purchased it from my godfather two years earlier. Therefore, this vehicle was in excellent condition, low miles and very attractive to sell. Actually, it was the only asset I owned that could generate cash, which is exactly what I needed if my college career was going to continue during the summer months. What was more important, my car or continuing my college education? My car of course! Since I engaged in a psychological contract with my parents, relatives, friends, and, more importantly myself. The written statement to me was more important than maintaining my only asset in life.

Well, it did not take long for me to start the process of selling my car. A quick sale is what I needed, mainly because summer school enrollment was quickly approaching. Luckily, I found a buyer for my car within one week, which allowed me time to register for summer school. I remember telling my brother that I sold my car and I was going back to school for the summer session. He stated, "I hope you know what you are doing." During the 1980's my brother considered God and cars as being on the same level.

With the car sold, I registered early and enrolled in three very tough classes. Enrolling in three classes instead of one was a gamble. I wanted to be prepared for the following year, just in case a similar situation presented itself.

As predicted, my second year of college seemed to mirror my first. I had to retake two classes if I wanted to maintain my schedule. With my goals in-hand, I was not going to let something or someone derail my scheduled graduation date. As the years continued my college experience revealed to me that not only were students not graduating within 4 years; they were leaving school at a rapid pace. I did not understand at the time that my goal was very aggressive for my environment.

Throughout the 4 years of college I spent working on my undergraduate degree; my written goals were a constant reminder of my sole purpose for going to school. My parents, relatives, and friends were also constant reminders of my obligation to myself. The psychological contract that originated from writing my goals on a sheet of paper and informing parents and associates was extremely strong; it kept me on track. My goal was to achieve a college degree within 4 years as I had scheduled. Graduating within 4 years, wow! Great accomplishment, BS degree. At this point in my life I realized that goal setting was a strict and powerful process. The process of writing goals on a sheet of paper had taken on a life of its own. I vowed to always devise a plan to set my goals year-after-year for the rest of my life.

As with most college graduates the next step was to find a job, or develop the perfect career path. I remember sitting at home and brainstorming how I was going to find a good job, I also recorded the information on a sheet of paper. I told my brother that I would be working for a major company within one year. He thought that I was crazy; he said one cannot work for a major company simply because he/she wrote it down on a sheet of paper. I informed him that my sheet of paper was a list of my annual goals, and written goals usually take on a life of their own. Well, he was not impressed, and he simply walked away shaking his head. Little did he know about the power of goal setting and the benefits it could offer.

As I started my job search, it included at least 200 resumes, within a 20-day time-period. Every letter that arrived in the mail that was addressed to me stated that my application would be on file for one year. The same letters were adding additional energy to my brother's discouragement. During my fourth month of searching for the perfect job, my brother stated, "You should probably revise your goals." I informed my brother that goals were something that you live with, a process of staying on course and giving 110%.

During my fifth month of searching, General Motors Corporation (GM) called to schedule an interview; once my interview was scheduled, I informed my family that I was going to be hired by GM. However, everyone did not understand why

I believed that getting hired by GM was an automatic process. It appears my brother finally understood, because he was telling everyone that would listen, "Don will be hired by GM because that is one of his goals for the year." As expected during the interview process, I behaved as if I was already offered the job. I displayed high energy, a positive attitude, and a feeling of belonging to the organization.

I believe my interviewer's perception of me was very positive. I think they absorbed and felt the positive energy coming from me. Therefore, when I was offered a job in the Salary / Hourly Payroll department I was not surprised. Writing my goals on a sheet of paper allowed me to believe in my theory. The theory of, "if you can see it, you'll believe it"! Writing goals on a sheet of paper is part of seeing whereas believing is something that starts with an idea.

During my years working for GM I began to establish my yearly goals. Each year I would establish and increase the difficulty of my previous goals. Achieving my yearly goals allowed me the opportunity to increase the level of difficulty. During my 21 years with GM I received 6 promotions, gained experience in 7 different divisions, and held 9 positions in total.

All possible because of the goal-setting exercise that I learned during the early years of my college experience.

While working for GM, I had the opportunity to enroll in and obtain my Masters and Doctoral degrees. As I established and re-arranged my yearly goals, I needed a challenge. Therefore, within 2 years of being out of college, I began a journey to obtain my Masters degree. Trying to obtain my Masters degree while working was challenging; however, I continued to set my goals, only this time I was establishing a schedule detailing the number of classes that I needed to complete on an annual basis. This process was very beneficial because it allowed me the opportunity to complete my Masters degree in two years. Two years! Wow! It was not a mark of an overachiever; it simply was the result of a structured process from a determined individual.

I allowed myself 2 years to accomplish the goal of obtaining a Masters degree. During this time period, the average graduate student was completing masters programs obtaining their degrees within 2 years. Therefore, it was only natural for me to establish an aggressive 2-year goal. My goal-setting practice was very structured during the 1990's; therefore, I was going to do everything within my power to accomplish my goal. I do mean everything; I was going to give a 110% effort. For example, I can remember walking all night in my living room reading a textbook. I was walking to keep from falling asleep. My strategy worked; with my dedication to my goals it appeared that I would be willing to do anything to succeed. "Failure was not an option."

As with my other goal-setting successes, I enlisted my parents, relatives, and friends to encourage me. Encourage me they did; however, I am not sure if they realized it was encouragement. It appeared that my two-year goal became a constant discussion item whenever I talked to my parents, relatives, and friends. Their constant reminders helped me stay on schedule; I was not going to retract my very aggressive goal of obtaining my Masters degree within 2 years.

With my detailed goal list, I planned every aspect of my 2-year plan. I planned for the financial crunch that was going to follow my enrollment into the Masters Degree program. I knew exactly how many classes I needed to complete annually. With my advanced planning and goal-setting contract, it was extremely easy to complete my Masters degree within two years. Wow! What an accomplishment, I completed my Masters degree as I had planned.

When someone asked me how I completed my Masters degree within 2 years I simply told them, it was possible through goal setting. As we know, goal setting is the process of specifying desired outcomes toward which individuals; teams, departments, and organizations will strive and is intended to increase organizational efficiency and effectiveness. My goal was not difficult, but it was achievable and challenging.

With my knowledge regarding goal setting, nothing frustrates me more than hearing someone say that they cannot accomplish something. When people state that something is not accomplishable, it indicates a lack of planning or taking action to set their goals. How can someone say something cannot be accomplished if they do not develop a plan or goal for action?

Another goal that I wanted to accomplish was to obtain a Doctorate degree. I wanted to accomplish this goal more than anything in life. Before I started the process to obtain a Doctorate degree, I completed my research. During my research regarding obtaining a Doctorate degree I uncovered some startling facts. For example, less than 20% of all people starting Doctoral degree programs actually finish. Of course, numerous factors could have been involved in this surprising statistic, such as, family issues, financial problems, accidents, and unforeseen natural disasters. The average Doctoral candidate's program lasted approximately 6-7 years. The goal of obtaining a Doctorate degree appeared to be a stressful task based on my initial findings; however, I learned very early in my life that, "If I could see it, I could believe it."

The process of developing an action plan and changing my thought process was easy, due to my past success with goal setting. I simply wrote my goals in a book, detailing my area of concentration, the numbers of years to complete this process, and what my future plans were once I obtained my Doctorate degree. Of course, I cannot minimize the effects regarding psychological contracts and pressure that I generated from people I partnered with. During my initial two years in the program I told anyone who would listen. My exact words were, "Have you heard, I have embarked on a journey to obtain my Doctorate degree." Of course a goal of this status would prompt people to ask many questions, which allowed me to hear my name attached to a Doctoral conversation. The psychological contract that I experienced was mind altering; it helped me to change my paradigm. With goal setting and a new thought process, I was truly becoming a Ph.D. It took a total of 5 years to achieve my dream of becoming a Ph.D., and throughout the 5 years my plan became more detailed. I would write all of my goals in detail; example, number of classes needed, financial resources needed, number of pages and ideas needed to complete my dissertation, and the number of colleagues needed to assist me with my goal.

The entire goal-setting process was very powerful; the discipline of writing and studying based on a contract with myself was inspirational. "Failure was not an option." I would view my written goal approximately 20 times per week. As I stated earlier, "If you see it, you will believe it." I truly believed that failure was not an option, especially during the tough times of re-drafting my dissertation. Re-drafting and revising became an ongoing process for two years; it appeared that there was no end to this process. However, my goal-setting worksheet continued to show me that obtaining my Doctorate degree was possible. It appears that most Doctoral candidates drop out of their programs during the dissertation writing phase. As I previously stated, my goals were very detailed; one of my goals regarding obtaining my Doctorate degree was, "Complete as many re-drafts or revisions to your dissertation as required". Therefore my committee and school could have told me to write re-drafts and revisions for 10 years instead of 2 years. My goal would not allow me to stop; I was going to do whatever it took to be successful. I think if more people wrote a fool proof plan regarding their expectation in trying to achieve something by investigating all scenarios, what could and can happen during their journey, achieving goals would be easy. Obtaining my Doctorate degree was easy, due to my detailed goal-setting process, and the fact that I wanted it more than a "drowning man wants air to survive!"

My last goal is current and ongoing; I want to become one of the best professors in my profession. During 1999 when I became an adjunct professor for a local college, one of my first goals was to become a great professor. One of the ways I started out to achieve this goal was to analyze all the best practices during my academic and business career. What was engaging and interesting regarding presenters, professors, and business partners? What was moving the emotions of people?

What were the best practices of the successful managers, professors, and business partners? My experience in these two areas helped me form successful strategies and techniques.

I believe it is very important to investigate and analyze all goals before attempting them. We must know our current status before we can predict the outcome. These strategies and techniques developed during the early years of my career are still true today. My evaluations from students and peers have not changed over the years. Students and peers believe that I am one of the best professors that they have ever encountered. The consistency in my evaluations over the years has occurred because of my continuous effort to include the goal of always striving to become a great professor. My annual goal of becoming the best professor possible is consistent with the person I want to become. I need to do whatever it takes to become the best professor in my profession. I need to see this goal on paper every day to remind myself of my purpose in life. It helps that I have a Type A Personality. I have a high energy level, I always feel a need to improve, and I love to achieve goals.

Whenever I am in the classroom I give students 110% of my knowledge and effort. I believe that professors cannot turn a switch "on and off" giving some subjects 70% and others 110%; the switch needs to be "turned on high" all of the time. That's probably why my students have received an abundance of knowledge while attending my classes. Setting a goal of being one of the best professors also involves a big responsibility. The responsibility of ensuring that every student learns and becomes successful in her or his life is very important. Ultimately, if you are teaching students, it is your job to ensure their success in mastering the subject. Ensuring student success could involve assigning extra homework, extra hours of instruction or assigning a student tutor. Giving 110% truly means taking full responsibility for yourself and the education of your students.

<u>Goal Achievement Questionnaire</u>

	Strongly Agree	Agree	Unsure	Disagree	Strongly Disagree
I am committed to my goals	—	—	—	—	—
I am willing to exert every effort to achieve my goals	—	—	—	—	—
I truly care about achieving my goals	—	—	—	—	—
I will gain personal satisfaction when I achieve my goals.	—	—	—	—	—
My expectations for my goals are realistic	—	—	—	—	—

Scouring: Give yourself 20 points for each Strongly Agree response; 15 points for each Agree response; 10 points for each Unsure response: 5 points for each Disagree response; and 0 points for each Strongly Disagree response. (The higher your total score, the greater possibility you have of achieving your goals)

Summary

This concludes the goal-setting Goal Setting exercise. Once all sections of this book have been completed, specific goals should be clearly defined.

Goals allow your targets to be achieved; however, first you must know your targets. Whenever the opportunity arises for you to attempt something, do not hesitate to utilize the goal-setting Goal Setting. This book will ensure a clear path of action that will allow you to monitor your progress in an attempt to accomplish your goals.

Whenever a situation occurs where you are uncertain of your projected goals, simply look at the contract you signed with yourself. Your signature on this document will reaffirm your agreement to yourself and to your future. Remember, a quitter never wins and a winner never quits. Therefore, when you accomplish your goals, you are winning in the game of life.

Utilize the Goal Setting faithfully, and the task of accomplishing goals will become effortless.

Goal Setting

CONFIDENCE + GOALS = SUCCESS

$$C + G = S$$

My Goal Setting Journal
Year 1

_____

_____

_____

_____

_____

_____

_____

_____

_____

_____

_____

_____

_____

_____

_____

_____

_____

_____

My Goal Setting Journal
Year 2

_____

_____

_____

_____

_____

_____

_____

_____

_____

_____

_____

_____

_____

_____

_____

_____

_____

_____

_____

My Goal Setting Journal
Year 3

_____

_____

_____

_____

_____

_____

_____

_____

_____

_____

_____

_____

_____

_____

_____

_____

_____

_____

My Goal Setting Journal
Year 4

_____

_____

_____

_____

_____

_____

_____

_____

_____

_____

_____

_____

_____

_____

_____

_____

_____

_____

_____

My Goal Setting Journal
Year 5

_____

_____

_____

_____

_____

_____

_____

_____

_____

_____

_____

_____

_____

_____

_____

_____

_____

_____

CPSIA information can be obtained
at www.ICGtesting.com
Printed in the USA
FSOW01n1537120317
31825FS